BOOK ANALYSIS

Written by Mélanie Ackerman and Apolline Boulanger

Translated by Rebecca Neal

Exit the King
BY EUGÈNE IONESCO

Bright
≡Summaries.com

EUGÈNE IONESCO

FRENCH DRAMATIST

- **Born in Slatina (Romania) in 1909.**
- **Died in Paris in 1994.**
- **Notable works:**
  - *The Bald Soprano* (1950), play
  - *The Lesson* (1951), play
  - *Rhinoceros* (1959), play

Born to a Romanian father and a French mother, Eugène Ionesco arrived in France as an infant and was made a French citizen in 1951. Although he was born in 1909, he always claimed he was born in 1912 to make himself appear younger. His theatrical works (such as *The Bald Soprano*; *The Lesson*; *The Chairs*, 1952) left their mark on literature: today, he is one of the most performed French dramatists in the world. He wanted to make sure his works were understood, so he wrote many commentaries on them (including *Notes and Counter Notes*, 1962; *Fragments of a Journal*, 1967). He was elected to the Académie française in 1970.

Ionesco was the leading figure of the Theatre of The Absurd, a new theatrical genre which rewrote the rules of classical theatre in the aftermath of the Second World War (1939-1945).

EXIT THE KING

AN UNCONVENTIONAL PLAY

- **Genre:** play
- **Reference edition:** Ionesco, E. (1994) *Exit the King, The Killer, Macbett*. Trans. Marowitz, C. and Watson, D. New York: Grove Press.
- **1st edition:** 1962
- **Themes:** anxiety, death, destiny, royalty, marriage

The single-act play *Exit the King* was published in 1962. The fact that the title alone sums up its plot (in French this is even clearer: the title is *Le roi se meurt*, or "The King Dies") highlights the fact that Ionesco is on the margins of the theatre and rejects traditional writing, like other representatives of the Theatre of the Absurd. This characteristic can be seen throughout the play, especially in its structure, and particularly at the beginning.

The play depicts King Berenger's reaction to the fact that he will die in just over an hour. Although initially he struggles to believe or accept this, he ultimately becomes aware of this reality and comes to terms with it, with the help of other characters. By depicting the death of the protagonist, the author does more than simply tell the story of a man's destiny; he illustrates the path towards decline that we will all go down.

SUMMARY

A KINGDOM IN DIFFICULTY

The royal palace is facing its first problems. The elements are growing rebellious: in particular, the sun now refuses to give out heat. The two queens are worried about this. Queen Marie is also overcome with sadness at the idea of losing her husband, King Berenger the First. The king is plagued by a range of illnesses whose origins he does not understand. Although he has always been aware of the finality of death, he still does not realise that it will soon be upon him. His first wife, Queen Marguerite, tries to reason with Marie, telling her that crying will not change anything. She says that it is far better to act for the good of the king, the kingdom and the people by remaining stoical and agreeing to tell Berenger the truth about his condition.

The doctor of the kingdom then offers his opinion: the decline in the king's health and his impending death are inevitable, and hope is useless. A general decline is confirmed by the collision of Mars and Saturn, and by earthquakes. The kingdom is also falling apart: there are no more ministers, there are less and less children in the schools, and the earth is becoming sterile and beginning to crack.

AN IMMINENT DEATH

When he learns that his death is imminent, the king, who refuses to see his power decline or his state become weaker, tries to give orders that nobody follows any more. In addition, he pretends that he is getting better. Berenger is suddenly aware of what lies in wait for him and becomes scared. Queen Marguerite tells him that he should have prepared for death a little bit each day, and he replies that he thought about it without actually doing it. He is frightened and calls for the people to help him, but he is gradually stripped of his power against his will, while the members of his court start to be overcome by emotion. However, Marguerite remains very dignified and admonishes those around her. She laments this situation which stops the king from making progress; according to her, all he does is complain. In a burst of courage, Queen Marie asks the king to be clear-headed and to stay strong, before breaking down in tears again.

Those around Berenger appeal to the natural elements in order to help the king, as they are no longer capable of doing anything themselves. After trying to conceal his condition and appear healthy, the king collapses into a wheelchair brought by his servant Juliette. While talking to her, he realises the work she has done and the kind of life he has given her. He gradually becomes nostalgic for the events of life, no matter how trivial (for example, he becomes attached to the idea of beef stew) or unhappy. It is only when he accepts letting go of life that his fear leaves him and he can think about death.

ACCEPTANCE

The doctor offers the following diagnosis: "He'll still be subject to fright, but pure fright, without abdominal complications. We can't hope this death will be an example to others. But it will be fairly respectable. His death will kill him now, and not his fear. We'll have to help him all the same". Queen Marguerite agrees to be present to help the king, while, now that her charm is becoming useless, Marie gradually loses her influence over him. Consequently, Berenger no longer pays attention to his wife or the words of hope she offers him. Now, death is the only thing on his mind.

While the king is still reminiscing about the past, the doctor becomes worried about the duration of his illness. The guard, meanwhile, talks about the memorable actions of a great man who is now only a shadow of his former self. The king begins to lose his memory and forgets who Marie is; Marguerite then gains the upper hand and claims that the king will leave the world with her image in his mind rather than that of the second queen. The characters gradually disappear. The king, who is now blind, is guided by his first wife. The kingdom reaches its end: the only people remaining are the king and Marguerite, who removes the obstacles in the ruler's last journey. Finally, the queen, the furniture and the other objects on stage disappear, followed shortly afterwards by Berenger.

CHARACTER STUDY

KING BERENGER THE FIRST

King Berenger is the play's central character, and the plot is constructed around his impending death. It is no coincidence that Ionesco chose the name Berenger: several of his characters have this name, including the protagonist of *Rhinoceros*. Ionesco has also stated that this detail allows him to stress the universality of death and turn his king into an everyman, facing the destiny that awaits us all. The king is narcissistic, selfish and immature, and it takes him a long time to realise, and then to accept, that he will die.

Throughout the play, we can observe a degradation and an awareness of his state which unfolds in several stages:

- **Degradation.** From the very beginning of the play, the viewer can see that the king is losing his power and authority: nothing works in his kingdom, the walls are cracking and everything is falling into ruin.
- **Denial.** We have to wait some time for his second appearance, which allows Berenger to prepare for the ceremony and talk about his increasingly close and inevitable death. He appears barefoot, and this grotesque detail offsets the tragic nature of the character. The king's speech, which is made up of short sentences and punctuated by tactless remarks (in particular towards Marguerite) reveals an irresponsible, selfish and immature man who has never really grown up: he places more importance on his good times and wellbeing than on the

urgent needs of the kingdom. He does not consider his illnesses as warning signs of death, but as a consequence of his growth: "Perhaps I've been growing!" The fact that Marie mothers him too much also reinforces the impression that the king is behaving like a child. When Marguerite tells him that he is going to die, he rejects this idea like a temperamental child, believing that his time has not yet come.

- **Awareness.** He then realises that his condition is worsening more and more quickly, and that death is not as far away as he had hoped: "My good people, I am going to die! Hear me! Your King is going to die!" However, this awareness is marked by fear: he appeals to the people for help and still thinks that he can escape his tragic end, seeking refuge by looking to the past: "(*To* MARIE:) I want to be a baby and you can be my mother". His fear makes him ready to do anything to avoid death: "Let every human creature die provided I can live forever".

- **Acceptance.** The king gradually manages to rid himself of his fear by sweating it out: the doctor says "It's panic oozing through his pores". From then on, as he comes to terms with his fate, the elements of life begin to disappear: Marie, who is also in denial about death, evaporates, and the guard, Juliette and the doctor leave suddenly. The king gradually loses his senses, and Marguerite helps him to release himself from the burden of life, until he has nothing left.

THE KING'S WIVES

The king has two wives, Marguerite and Marie. In an interview with the professor Paul Louis Mignon, Ionesco explained this bigamy by saying that, in his view, every man has two wives: life and death. They therefore symbolise the two components of existence.

Queen Marguerite

Marguerite is the king's first wife and belongs to the past. She has all the attributes appropriate to her rank but, unlike Queen Marie who is young and fresh, her style is drab and old-fashioned.

In a way, her inflexible character, firm words and the fact that she belongs to the past make her the embodiment of classical tragedy. Her role is to remind the king that he will die and to guide him towards the end of his final performance. She is the one who makes every effort to bring about the tragic ending, by removing the invisible strings that attach the king to life. She embodies reason and strictness, a has stopped hoping and believing in life.

She symbolises the tragic ending represented by death and fatality, and also serves as a sort of oracle by drawing on the doctor's observations: she is the one who announces the king's demise, calculates how much time he has left to live and helps him to fulfil his destiny by guiding him to his death and lifing all the burdens he has accumulated during his life. She seems to have the power to lead living things towards their end: Marie blames her for the death of the royal cat, because the old queen "hated that sentimental, timorous beast". She stands in opposition to the love and carefree nature of youth represented by Marie. The two wives maintain their rivalry throughout the entire play, trying to weigh up their power over the king: while one tries to make him listen to reason, the other wants to make him forget his suffering and give him hope.

Queen Marie

Marie is the king's youngest wife and, although she is his second queen, she is "first in affection". Indeed, she is the only one he feels genuine affection for. He is tired of seeing Marguerite, who symbolises reason and death, and prefers Marie, who embodies joie de vivre and carefreeness. Marguerite says of her: "Laugh or cry, that's all she can do".

Unlike Marguerite, she is well-dressed and wears jewellery, which makes her superficial and associates her with denial. Whereas Marguerite symbolises the past, death and the tragic ending of the play, Marie represents life and hope. She is often presented as a maternal figure, calling Berenger "poor little king", which makes her a more ambiguous character. By taking on the role of both wife and mother, Marie keeps the king in a childlike state. Ionesco's choice to give her the same name as Jesus' mother was deliberate: this name makes her and the king two biblical figures who are not realistic and whose place and existence the author questions. This would make Marie the one who gives life, while Marguerite represents the one who leads people to death.

THE CHORUS

According to Ionesco, the three characters of the guard, Juliette and the doctor symbolise the chorus, a central element of Greek tragedy. The chorus is made up of citizens, and its role is to help the audience to follow the action by presenting, announcing and summarising it. In this way, the doctor announces the action, the guard describes it and Juliette, who represents the people, brings news from outside.

The guard

The guard is the first character to appear on stage. He is a recurring character in the tragedy, and his only function is to obey the king and provide information. However, he can no longer perform his duty: from his first appearance, he appears out of breath, old and tired, unable to hold his halberd correctly. He is also the first character to stop obeying the king's orders.

When the play begins, the guard gives an initial report of the decline of the kingdom. In doing so, he could also represent the chorus of the prologue, which introduces both the action and the characters of the play in ancient and classical tragedies.

His role, which is to guard the door while announcing the actions of the various characters, is used to comic effect when his words solemnly describe the laughable actions of the characters: "Long live the King. *The* KING *falls down* [...] The King is down! The King is dying!"

Juliette

Juliette is the servant and nurse at the castle, forced to take on multiple duties because there are so few subjects. Her way of speaking (in the French version of the play, she uses English expressions such as "living room") presents her as a character who is removed from the tragic tradition. Indeed, she talks to her rulers in a fairly familiar way and turns out to be very close to them: for example, shortly before the end of the play she has a long conversation with the king during which the two characters are on equal footing.

She is part of the chorus because, in a way, she represents the people. She is also one of the few characters who can leave the castle and bring news of the outside world. Likewise, she represents the subject who has followed the king's orders all her life, even though he never made the effort to listen to her, believing himself to be superior.

The doctor

Like Juliette, the doctor is a man of the people and occupies several somewhat contradictory roles: he is a doctor, astrologer, executioner and bacteriologist. His role as an astrologer conflicts with his scientific beliefs, and his appearance brings to mind that of a wizard: "He looks like an astrologer and an executioner at one and the same time. On his head he is wearing a pointed hat with stars. He is dressed in red with a hood handing from the collar, and holding a great telescope".

Likewise, his duties as a doctor and an executioner are

polar opposites: he saves lives, but also takes them. Like Marguerite, he serves as an oracle, capable of reading the stars and thus confirming the king's imminent death. He also analyses the events unfolding on stage, listing the different physical and psychological stages the king will have to go through before he dies.

ANALYSIS

THE GENRE OF THE PLAY: (ANTI-)TRAGEDY

The tragic register

Exit the King can be viewed as a tragedy because it has several characteristics of this genre, in terms of both form and content:

- The play's subject is the fate of a royal character. This is a key trait of tragic characters, who often have noble and influential lineage. In this case, the king possesses many symbols of power, such as his crown, his sceptre, his kingdom and the court.
- The ending is tragic because the main character dies.
- There is a chorus, with characters who are typical of tragedies.
- The play takes the form of a long dialogue, interspersed with stage directions which provide additional explanations.

TRAGEDY

Here, we are using the term "tragedy" in its literary sense rather than its broader sense. The *Collins English Dictionary* defines tragedy as "a type of literature, especially drama, that is serious and sad, and often ends with the death of the main character".

A break with classical conventions

However, several elements indicate that the author is breaking with the traditions of classical theatre and going against the rules of tragedy.

Firstly, we can see that, from a formal point of view, the structure is not respected: while tragedies typically have five acts, this play only has one. The title also challenges the outline of the development of the action. A tragedy normally comprises an initial situation, a climax and a conclusion, which allow the plot to develop. In this case, the title immediately announces the conclusion of the play, which becomes the subject of the action. The only question that the reader or spectator is left with is how the king is going to die.

Furthermore, the rules of classical drama set out by Boileau (French writer, 1636-1711) in his *L'Art poétique* ("Poetic Art") are challenged:

- The rule of *vraisemblance* ("verisimilitude"), which means that the events depicted must be realistic, is flouted: although death is obviously a real phenomenon, other elements in the play are improbable. For example, the king is over 400 years old, and there are a series of anachronisms in the play: while the décor is "vaguely Gothic" and royal music like that of the reign of Louis XIV can be heard, modern terms such as "radiator" and "living room" are also used.
- The rule of *bienséance* ("propriety" or "decorum"), which essentially means not showing deaths on stage, is broken

from the title, which announces that the play will depict the death of the king.

- The rule of the three unities is not respected:
  - The play does not unfold over a 24-hour period, but in real time. This is indicated by Marguerite, who says that the king will die in an hour and a half.
  - Although the setting remains the same for the entire play, it cannot be situated spatially.
  - There is no real unity of action in the play: there is not a genuine plot, as both the reader and the spectator know that the play will end with the death of the king.
- The stage directions do more than simply tell the actors how to move: they become aesthetic objects in their own right. This is the case in particular with the first stage direction, which plays on style by using anaphora, meaning the repetition of a word or phrase at the beginning of consecutive clauses ("vaguely dilapidated, vaguely Gothic"). The final stage direction, which overshadows the characters' words, is also important: it describes how the characters gradually disappear from the stage, leaving behind nothing more than a grey light. Stage directions punctuate Marguerite's final speech, and have the last word after all the characters have disappeared.

A parody of tragedy

More than simply breaking with tragic conventions, Ionesco parodies tragedy in this play, in particular through his characters' actions. The king, the ultimate tragic character, is now left with only his title, as his state is falling apart. His actions are sometimes grotesque or farcical: he appears barefoot on stage, revealing the lowest and least noble part of his body, and drops his crown on multiple occasions. In particular, he is held up to ridicule as he gradually loses his strength and his authority:

> "GUARD: Long live the King! *The* KING *falls down*. The King is dying.
> MARIE: Long live the King! *The* KING *stands up with difficulty, helping himself with his scepter.*
> GUARD: Long live the King! *The* KING *falls down again*. The King is dead.
> MARIE: Long live the King! Long live the King!
> MARGUERITE: What a farce."

In this extract, the comedy of repetition emphasises the laughable and ridiculous aspect of the king, reinforced by the stage direction that "*This scene should be played like a tragic Punch and Judy show*".

Finally, in an attempt to go beyond a simple parody of the tragic register, the play shows an awareness that it will be performed. When Marguerite says to the king "you're going to die at the end of the show", or when she addresses the audience, she shows that she is aware that she is giving a performance.

Language

Language has a particular place in *Exit the King*. More than a mode of communication, we see that it is coded and does not represent a real, natural exchange between people: it is artifice.

First of all, we can see that the plot is driven by words rather than actions: the king's journey towards death is constantly described and influenced by the words of the characters. Marguerite indicates Marie and says "We must keep that woman quiet! She says anything that comes into her head. She's not to open her mouth again without our permission". Once Marguerite has said that the king is going to die, his death becomes inevitable. It is generally his first wife's voice that guides the king towards death, particularly during the conclusion.

Finally, language is used to better challenge reality when it is reduced to wordplay and parody:

> "KING: But I am the State.
> JULIETTE: And what a state the poor man's in!"

There is a strong tautological component: language folds in on itself and on its form, resulting in a reflection on language:

> "MARIE: Oh God!
> KING (*to* MARGUERITE): I won't have anyone upset her. And why did she say, 'Oh God?'
> MARGUERITE: It's an expression."

Language is therefore turned in on itself, towards its form, its aesthetic and the multiple meanings that some words can have, particularly in the case of homonyms. Ionesco examines form rather than meaning, turning away from reality and making situations absurd.

THE REPRESENTATION OF DEATH

The representation of death is central in this play, since even its title reveals the king's critical condition. The title is a simple phrase which indicates that the main actions of the play will be the king's "exit", both literal and metaphorical: he will exit not only the stage, but also life. Once again, Ionesco breaks with theatrical conventions by announcing with the title that an act prohibited by classical rules will be shown on stage.

A declining kingdom

Although death primarily affects the king, it is omnipresent in the play and corrupts the entire kingdom: for example, we are told that "The sun has lost between fifty and seventy-five percent of its strength", "The trees are sighing and dying" and "Twenty-five of our countrymen have been liquefied".

This degradation also affects the characters: the people are sick, and the king's last subjects are growing old. For example, the guard is tired and struggles to remain standing and hold his weapon, while Juliette has no equipment in good condition and so cannot do the housework in the castle to an acceptable standard.

Exploded temporality: the dissipation of life and the time of tragedy

Death is also symbolised by time. Time becomes tragic when Marguerite announces: "You're going to die in an hour and a half, you're going to die at the end of the show". As soon as this premonition is uttered, death seems inevitable for the king. From that point on, his subjects no longer seem able to obey him and submit to Marguerite, who here represents the king's destiny.

In addition, the notion of time in the play is fairly flexible: for example, it seems to move faster when the end is near. The king has no more time; it "has melted in his hands". He seems to age suddenly: "All at once, he looks fourteen centuries older". While Berenger's life has been long and joyful, his death is set to be sudden and painful: at the start of the play, he *rapidly crosses the stage*", but it is not long until he starts limping, and then is unable to move about unaided.

The different stages of death

Finally, we see that the king goes through different stages on the way to death (degradation, denial, awareness and acceptance). Death seems to be performed and organised: the characters talk about preparing for a "ceremony". The king will have to completely abdicate "governmentally", "morally" and "physically". This statement, delivered by Marguerite, already heralds the turn that events will take:

- The king's power disappears and his subjects no longer obey him. This is his governmental death.
- He abdicates morally by announcing that he is going to die.
- He gradually abdicates physically and loses his senses until everything disappears.

Anxiety about ageing and death

The play can be interpreted as a representation of anxiety about ageing and dying, having accomplished nothing and leaving nothing behind. For example, the king laments that he "Never had the time to get to know life".

Death causes anguish because it is inevitable: the king cannot push back the fateful hour. He then worries about the role he played during life, particularly during his conversation with Juliette in which he takes the time to get to know his subject.

We are all equal before death

When he becomes aware that his death is imminent, the king expresses regret over the mistakes and blameworthy actions he committed in the past. In particular, he is sorry that he did not listen to his people, who are symbolised here by Juliette, enough. The long dialogue between the characters shortly before the end of the play provides an excellent illustration of this.

> "JULIETTE: I get quite worn out, exhausted!
> KING: You ought to have told us.
> JULIETTE: I did tell you.
> KING: That's true. Such a lot has escaped my notice. I never got to know everything. I never went everywhere I could. My life could have been so full."

The king's situation here is universal and pessimistic: whether or not we are prepared for it, we are all destined to die from the day we are born. Beyond that, death leaves us exposed to face up to our lives, and makes us all equal. The fact that the king spends a long time walking with and talking to Juliette, his servant, clearly illustrates a change in his attitude: Berenger is demonstrating humility towards life and those around him. Social differences disappear, so the king is no longer just a king but a man among many others, facing up to the universal destiny of death.

During his progress towards death, the king learns to be humble and to become aware not of himself but of the truth by leaving behind pride, egocentrism and narcissism. Marguerite helps him in this:

> "He imagines he's everything! He thinks his existence is all existence. I'll have to drive that out of his head! [...] He's holding the whole kingdom in his hand. In miniature: on microfilm... in tiny grains. (*To the* KING:) That grain won't grow again, it's bad seed! They're all moldy! Drop them! Unclasp your fingers! [...] They were only dust."

Here we once again find the idea that all men are equal in the face of death: the trivial concerns of life no longer matter.

THE LOST HOPE OF MODERN MAN: A PESSIMISTIC UNIVERSE

The Theatre of the Absurd

Samuel Beckett (Irish writer, 1906-1989), Jean Genet (French writer, 1910-1986), Arthur Adamov (Russian-born French dramatist, 1908-1970) and Ionesco are the main representatives of a genre which broke away from traditional theatre and stories as they had been understood until that point. Although the Theatre of the Absurd reached its peak in the mid-20th century, the first traces of a theatre that broke away from the mainstream could be observed earlier.

The movement's authors indicated this break in their writing by rejecting generally accepted notions of plot and character. This often gave rise to senseless or absurd stories, which is where the name of the genre comes from. The best example of this is undoubtedly Ionesco's *The Bald Soprano*, which recounts a conversation between several characters without any semblance of a plot. The dialogue does not follow any logic, providing a fine demonstration of the absurd in theatre.

The influence of the First World War on the arts

The brutality of the First World War (1914-1918) left profound mental and emotional scars. This can be seen in a range of art forms, such as poetry and painting. It also affected literature, as can be seen in numerous movements which were the forerunners of the Theatre of the Absurd. In particular, in the immediate aftermath of the war, Dada, introduced by Tristan Tzara (Romanian-born French writer, 1896-1963) and Surrealism, led by André Breton (French writer, 1896-1966), demonstrated a desire to break away from the mainstream. They opposed tradition, which had failed during the tragic years of conflict: reality was rejected.

In *Exit the King*, absurdity comes from the removal of plot. Indeed, we can even say that the plot does not exist, because the title and beginning of the play leave no doubt as to how it will unfold. The reflections on language reinforce the absurdity of the conversation and the play as a whole. Words and expressions no longer have clear meanings, which means that the characters can no longer understand and communicate with one another.

Dehumanisation

The play therefore reveals a loss of hope in humanity. After two world wars and the advent of the Cold War, humanity seemed to be lost. The characters no longer have their own identities, but are more like embodiments of particular types. In this way, the king represents the everyman: "He extinguished volcanoes and caused new ones to erupt. He built Rome [...] He wrote tragedies and comedies, under the name of Shakespeare". He is the world; he is man in his entirety. The fact that he is compared to Shakespeare is no coincidence: his death therefore corresponds to the death of the theatre of the past. By giving him several identities, Ionesco makes Berenger an everyman who is dying and has no real identity. He is only character and performance.

Marguerite represents death and Marie life, while the three other characters represent the people. Every trace of individuality has been erased. They are a caricature of the bygone age of tragedy and describe themselves as taking part in a performance:

> "[I am] like an actor on the first night who doesn't know his lines and who dries, dries, dries [...] I don't know this audience, and I don't want to. I've nothing to say to them. What a state I'm in!"

Here, the characters are only present as characters, and function as puppets rather than real people.

The loss of hope in God

As well as a loss of hope in humanity, Ionesco's play also conveys the beginnings of a loss of hope in God. The king can be compared to God, who is abandoning his subjects (humanity as a whole), taking comfort in decline and in a form of narcissism:

> "I see myself. Behind everything, I exist. Nothing but me everywhere. I am the earth, I am the sky, I am the wind, I am the fire: am I in every mirror or am I the mirror of everything?"

Consequently, the king can be compared to a divinity, especially as everything around him is progressively destroyed in parallel with his death: the kingdom is devastated, all his subjects flee or perish, and even the universe seems to be in crisis (the stars and the comets collide). The fact that his wife Marie treats him like a child also means that the two characters can be compared to the Virgin Mary and her son Jesus. However, they do not communicate authentic values and are in denial: just like the king, Marie refuses to see death coming. Their mistaken position also raises questions about the place of God, who, obsessed by himself, does not see the chaos which prevails among his subjects and is therefore left powerless.

Exit the King therefore parodies the methods of classical theatre, in particular by mixing the tragic and the comic. Through the character of Berenger, Ionesco draws up a sort of list of the reactions man can have to death. By rejecting verisimilitude and realism, he demonstrates both the tragic destiny of humankind and the loss of hope in a better world.

FURTHER REFLECTION

SOME QUESTIONS TO THINK ABOUT...

- In the opening section of the play, what elements show that the genre of tragedy is being distorted?
- In your opinion, what effects might a play like this have had on audiences at the time? Would a contemporary reader or spectator react differently?
- Has the Theatre of the Absurd put an end to the genre of tragedy? Explain your answer.
- How would you describe the character of Marguerite and her role in the story?
- The distribution of speech at the end of the story differs from the rest of the play. How would you explain this?
- Comment on the following quotation from the play: "KING: Kings ought to be immortal. MARGUERITE: They are. Provisionally."
- Comment on the following quotation from the play: "Life can never be bad. It's a contradiction."
- Before the play was published, Ionesco had thought about giving it the title *The Ceremony*. How could this title be justified? In your opinion, why did Ionesco ultimately opt for the title *Exit the King*?
- Do you think that a play like this could have been written before the 20th century? Justify your answer.
- In an interview with the literary critic Claude Bonnefoy, Ionesco said: "It is death that closes a life, a play, a work. Otherwise, there is no ending. Finding an ending means simplifying theatre. If there needs to be an ending, it is

because the spectators need to go to bed"[1]. Comment on this remark in relation to the play.

- What parallels can be established between the condition of Berenger the First and the condition of language in the play? Develop your answer.

---

1. This quotation has been translated by BrightSummaries.com.

We want to hear from you!
Leave a comment on your online library
and share your favourite books on social media!

FURTHER READING

REFERENCE EDITION

- Ionesco, I. (1994) *Exit the King, The Killer, Macbett*. Trans. Marowitz, C. and Watson, D. New York: Grove Press.

MORE FROM BRIGHTSUMMARIES.COM

- Reading guide – *Rhinoceros* by Eugène Ionesco.
- Reading guide – *The Bald Soprano* by Eugène Ionesco.

Bright
≡Summaries.com

www.brightsummaries.com

Ebook EAN: 9782806295583

Paperback EAN: 9782806297150

Legal Deposit: D/2017/12603/253

This guide was written with the collaboration of Apolline Boulanger for the chapters 'Character study', 'A break with classical conventions', 'A parody of tragedy', 'Language', 'The representation of death', 'Dehumanisation' and 'The loss of hope in God'.

Cover: © Primento

Digital conception by Primento, the digital partner of publishers.

This guide was produced with the support of the *Service Général des Lettres et du Livre* of the Wallonia-Brussels Federation.